Slow Cooker
Recipes

pil
Publications
International Ltd.

Favorite Brand Name Recipes at www.fbnr.com

Vice President, Campbell's Kitchen
Lucinda Ayers
Group Manager, Campbell's Kitchen
Catherine Marschean-Spivak
Senior Manager, Campbell's Kitchen
Jane Freiman
Assistant Manager
Donna Liotto-Scocozza
Product Specialist
Erin Garvey

Pictured on the front cover: Beef Bourguignonne (page 72).

Pictured on the back cover (clockwise from top): Golden Chicken with Noodles (page 16), Slow Cooker Chicken & Dumplings (page 66), Chicken in Creamy Sun-Dried-Tomato Sauce (page 10), and Southwestern Chicken & White Bean Soup (page 32).

ISBN-13: 987-1-4127-2181-3
ISBN-10: 1-4127-2181-4

Manufactured in China.

8 7 6 5 4 3 2 1

Microwave Cooking: Microwave ovens vary in wattage. Use the cooking times as guidelines and check for doneness before adding more time.

Preparation/Cooking Times: Preparation times are based on the approximate amount of time required to assemble the recipe before cooking, baking, chilling, or serving. These times include preparation steps such as measuring, chopping, and mixing. The fact that some preparation and cooking can be done simultaneously is taken into account. Preparation of optional ingredients and serving suggestions is not included.

Campbell's®

Contents

Time to Savor   6
*The fastest way to save time in
the kitchen*

Supper's Ready   8
No-wait meals for busy weeknights

Winter Chill Chasers   26
*Wonderful ways to warm up
blustery days*

Heritage Recipes   50
Classic favorites made simple

A World of Flavor   70
*Slow cooking with an international
flair*

Index   92

12

64

86

Slow cooking is the fastest way
to save time in the kitchen

Time
to

Many cooks have already discovered that using a slow cooker is the fastest way to get a home-cooked meal on the table, especially on hectic weeknights! That may sound like a contradiction, but saving time—and giving you extra time to savor—is the best benefit of slow cooking.

Preparation is usually pretty simple. You can even do most of it the night before. Assemble the ingredients (either in the crockery liner of your slow cooker or in a bowl), cover, and store overnight in the refrigerator. In the morning, simply pop the ingredients into the slow cooker and set it before you set off on your busy day.

Cooking in the slow cooker also requires minimal attention. No supervising, no stirring, no scorching—just the pleasure of coming home to a home-cooked meal that's piping hot and ready to serve. It's also exceptionally delicious, because there's nothing like the slow cooker for mingling flavors and creating something really worth savoring. Thanks to the ease and convenience of the slow cooker, you'll have plenty of time to do just that!

Savor

Chicken in Creamy Sun-Dried-Tomato Sauce
Recipe on page 10

Supper's Ready

It's 6:00 p.m. The whole family—ravenously hungry and ready to eat—is finally home, including the chef (you), who just walked in the door along with everyone else. Good thing you thought ahead and started your slow cooker in the morning. What a fast, easy way to say "supper's ready!"

Slow cooking lends itself especially well to meal-in-one recipes that only require the addition of a salad and some bread or rolls to round out the menu—like this collection of ten easy weeknight dishes. While you go about your business during the day, your slow cooker is hard at work. So as soon as you return, there's a satisfying supper waiting that's ready when you are.

Chicken in Creamy Sun-Dried-Tomato Sauce

(pictured on page 8)

Prep Time: 15 minutes
Cook Time: 7 to 8 hours

2 cans (10¾ ounces **each**) Campbell's® Condensed Cream of Chicken Soup with Herbs

1 cup Chablis **or** other dry white wine*

¼ cup coarsely chopped pitted kalamata **or** oil-cured olives

2 tablespoons drained capers

2 cloves garlic, minced

1 can (14 ounces) artichoke hearts, drained and chopped

1 cup drained, coarsely chopped sun-dried tomatoes

8 skinless, boneless chicken breast halves (about 2 pounds)

½ cup chopped fresh basil leaves (optional)

Hot cooked rice, egg noodles **or** seasoned mashed potatoes

MIX soup, wine, olives, capers, garlic, artichokes and tomatoes in 3½-quart slow cooker. Add chicken and turn to coat.

COVER and cook on LOW 7 to 8 hours** or until chicken is no longer pink. Sprinkle with basil, if desired. Serve with rice, noodles or potatoes.

Serves 8.

*Substitute Swanson® Chicken Broth for the wine.

**Or on HIGH 4 to 5 hours

Weekday Pot Roast & Vegetables

Prep Time: 15 minutes
Cook Time: 10 to 12 hours
Stand Time: 10 minutes

2- to 2½-pound boneless beef bottom round **or** chuck pot roast

1 teaspoon garlic powder

1 tablespoon vegetable oil

4 medium potatoes (about 1 pound), each cut into 6 wedges

3 cups fresh **or** frozen baby carrots

1 medium onion, thickly sliced (about ¾ cup)

2 teaspoons dried basil leaves, crushed

2 cans (10¼ ounces **each**) Campbell's® Beef Gravy

SPRINKLE all sides of roast with garlic powder. Heat oil in medium skillet over medium-high heat. Add roast and cook until browned.

PLACE potatoes, carrots and onion in 3½-quart slow cooker. Sprinkle with basil. Top with roast. Pour gravy over roast and vegetables.

COVER and cook on LOW 10 to 12 hours* or until roast is fork-tender.

REMOVE roast from cooker and let stand 10 minutes. Serve roast with vegetables and gravy.

Serves 6 to 8.

*Or cook on HIGH 5 to 6 hours

TIP:
Browning the meat on the stovetop before adding it to the slow cooker adds to the flavor and color of the dish.

Slow-Cooked Pulled Pork Sandwiches

Prep Time: 15 minutes
Cook Time: 8 to 10 hours
Stand Time: 10 minutes

  1 tablespoon vegetable oil

     3½- to 4-pound boneless pork shoulder roast, netted **or** tied (Boston butt)

  1 can (10½ ounces) Campbell's® Condensed French Onion Soup

  1 cup ketchup

  ¼ cup cider vinegar

  3 tablespoons packed brown sugar

12 round sandwich rolls, split

HEAT oil in medium skillet over medium-high heat. Add roast and cook until browned. Place roast in 5-quart slow cooker.

MIX soup, ketchup, vinegar and brown sugar. Pour over roast.

COVER and cook on LOW 8 to 10 hours* or until roast is fork-tender.

REMOVE roast from cooker and let stand 10 minutes. Shred pork, using 2 forks. Return pork to cooker. Divide pork mixture and sauce among rolls.

Makes 12 sandwiches.

*Or on HIGH 4 to 5 hours

TIP:
Complement this Southern-style sandwich favorite with store-bought cole slaw and dill pickles.

Orange Chicken with Green Onions and Walnuts

Prep Time: 10 minutes
Cook Time: 8 to 9 hours

1½ cups Swanson® Chicken **or** Natural Goodness™ Chicken Broth

¼ cup teriyaki sauce

3 cloves garlic, minced

¾ cup orange marmalade

4 green onions, sliced (about ½ cup)

2 tablespoons cornstarch

8 skinless chicken thighs (about 2 pounds)

½ cup walnut pieces

Hot cooked rice

MIX broth, teriyaki sauce, garlic, marmalade, **¼ cup** green onions and cornstarch in 6-quart slow cooker. Add chicken and turn to coat.

COVER and cook on LOW 8 to 9 hours* or until chicken is no longer pink. Sprinkle with walnuts and remaining green onions before serving. Serve with rice.

Serves 8.

*Or on HIGH 4 to 5 hours

TIP:
Resist peeking! Every time the slow cooker lid is lifted, heat escapes—and 15 to 20 minutes will need to be added to the total cooking time.

Golden Chicken with Noodles

Prep Time: 5 minutes
Cook Time: 7 to 8 hours

2 cans (10¾ ounces **each**) Campbell's® Condensed Cream of Chicken **or** 98% Fat Free Cream of Chicken Soup

½ cup water

¼ cup lemon juice

1 tablespoon Dijon-style mustard

1½ teaspoons garlic powder

8 large carrots, thickly sliced (about 6 cups)

8 skinless, boneless chicken breast halves (about 2 pounds)

Hot cooked egg noodles

Chopped fresh parsley

MIX soup, water, lemon juice, mustard, garlic powder and carrots in 3½-quart slow cooker. Add chicken and turn to coat.

COVER and cook on LOW 7 to 8 hours* or until chicken is no longer pink. Serve with noodles. Sprinkle with parsley.

Serves 8.

Or on HIGH 4 to 5 hours

TIP:
Colors in slow-cooked food tend to fade, so add garnishes such as chopped fresh parsley just before serving.

Golden Mushroom Pork & Apples

Prep Time: 10 minutes
Cook Time: 8 to 9 hours

2 cans (10¾ ounces **each**) Campbell's® Condensed Golden Mushroom Soup

½ cup water

1 tablespoon packed brown sugar

1 tablespoon Worcestershire sauce

1 teaspoon dried thyme leaves, crushed

8 boneless pork chops, ¾-inch thick (about 2 pounds)

4 large Granny Smith apples, sliced

2 large onions, sliced (about 2 cups)

MIX soup, water, brown sugar, Worcestershire and thyme in 3½-quart slow cooker. Add pork, apples and onions.

COVER and cook on LOW 8 to 9 hours* or until pork is no longer pink.

Serves 8.

*Or on HIGH 4 to 5 hours

TIP:
To make cleanup easier, spray the inside of your slow cooker crock with vegetable cooking spray before adding the food.

Creamy Chicken & Wild Rice

Prep Time: 10 minutes
Cook Time: 7 to 8 hours

2 cans (10¾ ounces **each**) Campbell's® Condensed Cream of Chicken **or** 98% Fat Free Cream of Chicken Soup

1½ cups water

4 large carrots, thickly sliced (about 3 cups)

1 package (6 ounces) seasoned long-grain and wild rice mix

8 skinless, boneless chicken breast halves (about 2 pounds)

MIX soup, water, carrots and rice and seasoning packet in 3½-quart slow cooker. Add chicken and turn to coat.

COVER and cook on LOW 7 to 8 hours* or until chicken is no longer pink.

Serves 8.

Or on HIGH 4 to 5 hours

TIP:
Serve with fresh broccoli steamed in Swanson® Chicken Broth for extra flavor.

Nacho Chicken & Rice Wraps

Prep Time: 5 minutes
Cook Time: 7 to 8 hours

2 cans (10¾ ounces **each**) Campbell's® Condensed Cheddar Cheese Soup

1 cup water

2 cups Pace® Chunky Salsa **or** Picante Sauce

1¼ cups **uncooked** regular long-grain white rice*

2 pounds skinless, boneless chicken breasts, cut into cubes

10 flour tortillas (10-inch), warmed

MIX soup, water, salsa, rice and chicken in 3½-quart slow cooker.

COVER and cook on LOW 7 to 8 hours** or until chicken is no longer pink.

SPOON about **1 cup** rice mixture down center of each tortilla. Fold tortilla around filling.

Serves 10.

*For firmer rice, substitute converted rice for regular.

**Or on HIGH 4 to 5 hours

Melt-in-Your-Mouth Short Ribs

Prep Time: 10 minutes
Cook Time: 8 to 10 hours

3 pounds beef short ribs

2 tablespoons packed brown sugar

3 cloves fresh garlic, minced

1 teaspoon dried thyme leaves, crushed

¼ cup all-purpose flour

1 can (10½ ounces) Campbell's® Condensed French Onion Soup

1 bottle (12 fluid ounces) dark ale **or** beer

Hot mashed potatoes **or** buttered noodles

PLACE beef, brown sugar, garlic and thyme in 3½- to 6-quart slow cooker. Sprinkle with flour and toss to coat.

MIX soup and ale. Pour over beef.

COVER and cook on LOW 8 to 10 hours* or until beef is fork-tender. Remove beef from sauce. Spoon off fat from sauce before serving. Serve with potatoes or noodles.

Serves 6.

*Or on HIGH 4 to 5 hours

Southwestern Bean Medley

Prep Time: 10 minutes
Cook Time: 7 to 8 hours

1 can (14 ounces) Swanson® Vegetable Broth

1 tablespoon chili powder

1 teaspoon ground cumin

1 can (about 16 ounces) black beans, rinsed and drained

1 can (about 16 ounces) chickpeas (garbanzo beans), rinsed and drained

1 can (about 16 ounces) white kidney (cannellini) beans, rinsed and drained

½ cup dried lentils

1 can (14½ ounces) diced tomatoes and green chilies

Chopped fresh cilantro leaves

MIX broth, chili powder, cumin, black beans, chickpeas, white kidney beans and lentils in 3½-quart slow cooker.

COVER and cook on LOW 6 to 7 hours*.

ADD tomatoes. Cover and cook for 1 hour. Sprinkle with cilantro.

Serves 8.

Or on HIGH 4 to 5 hours

TIP:
For a complete meal, serve over hot cooked rice.

Creamy Chicken Tortilla Soup
Recipe on page 28

Wonderful ways to warm up blustery days

Winter Chill Chasers

It's only natural. When the thermometer drops, we want lots of homey, satisfying foods like soups and stews to lift our spirits and warm us up. Brimming with wholesome ingredients and the kind of delicious, mingled flavors that only come from long, slow simmering, they bring comfort by the bowlful.

These Campbell's slow cooker recipes make it easy and convenient to fix hearty, meal-in-a-bowl main dishes, even if you have other things to do on a winter's day. They can simmer unsupervised in your kitchen for hours. Then, when it's time to eat, all you have to do is ladle out a big, steaming bowl for everyone, shut the door against the chill, and settle in. Ahhhh!

Creamy Chicken Tortilla Soup

(pictured on page 26)

Prep Time: 10 minutes
Cook Time: 5 hours 30 minutes

½ cup chopped red pepper

½ cup diced tomato

1 can (8¾ ounces) whole kernel corn, drained

½ pound skinless, boneless chicken breasts, cut into ½-inch pieces

1 can (10¾ ounces) Campbell's® Condensed Chicken Verde Soup

1½ cups water

2 corn tortillas (6-inch), cut into strips

½ cup shredded Cheddar cheese (2 ounces)

¼ cup chopped fresh cilantro leaves

PLACE pepper, tomato, corn and chicken in 3½-quart slow cooker.

MIX soup and water. Pour over chicken mixture.

COVER and cook on LOW 5 hours*.

ADD tortillas, cheese and cilantro. Cover and cook for 30 minutes. Serve with additional cheese, if desired.

Serves 4.

*Or on HIGH 2 to 2 ½ hours

Beef & Vegetable Soup

Prep Time: 25 minutes
Cook Time: 8 to 10 hours

 1 pound beef for stew, cut into 1-inch pieces

    Ground black pepper

 2 tablespoons all-purpose flour

 2 tablespoons vegetable oil

 3 large onions, chopped (about 3 cups)

12 small red-skinned potatoes, cut into quarters

 2 medium carrots, sliced (about 1 cup)

 4 cloves garlic, minced

 1 tablespoon chopped fresh thyme **or** 1 teaspoon dried thyme leaves,
    crushed

 1 box (32 ounces) Swanson® Beef **or** Lower Sodium Beef Broth

 2 tablespoons tomato paste

1½ teaspoons instant coffee powder **or** granules

    Sour cream (optional)

    Chopped green onions (optional)

SPRINKLE beef with black pepper and coat with flour. Heat oil in medium skillet over medium-high heat. Add beef and cook until browned, stirring often.

PLACE onions, potatoes, carrots, garlic and thyme in 3½-quart slow cooker. Top with beef. Mix **1 cup** broth, tomato paste and coffee. Pour coffee mixture and remaining broth into cooker.

COVER and cook on LOW 8 to 10 hours* or until beef is fork-tender. Serve with sour cream and green onions, if desired.

Serves 6.

*Or on HIGH 4 to 5 hours

Barley and Lentil Soup

Prep Time: 10 minutes
Cook Time: 8 to 9 hours

2 boxes (32 ounces **each**) Swanson® Beef **or** Lower Sodium Beef Broth
   (8 cups)

2 cloves garlic, minced

1 teaspoon dried oregano leaves, crushed

4 large carrots, sliced (about 3 cups)

1 large onion, chopped (about 1 cup)

½ cup dried lentils

½ cup **uncooked** barley

MIX broth, garlic, oregano, carrots, onion, lentils and barley in 3½- to 6-quart slow cooker.

COVER and cook on LOW 8 to 9 hours* or until tender.

Serves 8.

*Or on HIGH 4 to 5 hours

Southwestern Chicken & White Bean Soup

Prep Time: 15 minutes
Cook Time: 8 to 10 hours

1 tablespoon vegetable oil

1 pound skinless, boneless chicken breasts, cut into 1-inch pieces

1 can (14 ounces) Swanson® Chicken **or** Natural Goodness™ Chicken Broth (1¾ cups)

1 cup Pace® Chunky Salsa

3 cloves garlic, minced

2 teaspoons ground cumin

1 can (about 16 ounces) small white beans, rinsed and drained

1 cup frozen whole kernel corn

1 large onion, chopped (about 1 cup)

HEAT oil in medium skillet over medium-high heat. Add chicken and cook until browned, stirring often.

MIX broth, salsa, garlic, cumin, beans, corn and onion in 3½-quart slow cooker. Top with chicken.

COVER and cook on LOW 8 to 10 hours* or until chicken is no longer pink.

Serves 6.

*Or on HIGH 4 to 5 hours

Veal Stew with Garden Vegetables

Prep Time: 10 minutes
Cook Time: 8 to 10 hours

2- to 2½-pounds veal for stew, cut into 1-inch pieces*

Ground black pepper

2 tablespoons olive oil

1 bag (16 ounces) fresh **or** frozen whole baby carrots (about 2½ cups)

1 large onion, diced (about 1 cup)

4 cloves garlic, minced

¼ cup all-purpose flour

2 cups Swanson® Chicken **or** Natural Goodness™ Chicken Broth

½ teaspoon dried rosemary leaves, crushed

1 can (about 14½ ounces) diced tomatoes

1 cup frozen peas

Hot cooked rice **or** barley

SPRINKLE veal with black pepper.

HEAT oil in saucepot. Add veal in 2 batches and cook until browned, stirring often.

PLACE veal, carrots, onion and garlic in 3½- to 6-quart slow cooker. Sprinkle with flour and toss to coat.

ADD broth, rosemary and tomatoes.

COVER and cook on LOW 7 to 8 hours**.

ADD peas. Cover and cook for 1 hour or until veal is fork-tender. Serve over rice or barley.

Serves 6.

*Substitute skinless, boneless chicken thighs, cut into 1-inch pieces, for veal.

Or on **HIGH 4 to 5 hours

Slow-Simmered Chicken Rice Soup

Prep Time: 15 minutes
Cook Time: 7 to 8 hours

½ cup **uncooked** wild rice

½ cup **uncooked** regular long-grain white rice

1 tablespoon vegetable oil

3 cans (14 ounces **each**) Swanson® Chicken **or** Natural Goodness™ Chicken Broth (5¼ cups)

2 teaspoons dried thyme leaves, crushed

¼ teaspoon crushed red pepper

2 stalks celery, coarsely chopped (about 1 cup)

1 medium onion, chopped (about ½ cup)

1 pound skinless, boneless chicken breasts, cut into cubes

Sour cream (optional)

Chopped green onions (optional)

MIX wild rice, white rice and oil in 3½-quart slow cooker. Cover and cook on HIGH 15 minutes.

ADD broth, thyme, red pepper, celery, onion and chicken to cooker. Turn heat to LOW. Cover and cook on LOW 7 to 8 hours* or until chicken is no longer pink. Serve with sour cream and green onions, if desired.

Serves 8.

*Or on HIGH 4 to 5 hours

TIP:
Speed preparation by substituting 3 cans (5 ounces **each**) Swanson® Premium Chunk Chicken instead of the raw poultry.

White Bean with Fennel Soup

Prep Time: 15 minutes
Cook Time: 7 to 8 hours

  1 box (32 ounces) Swanson® Organic Vegetable Broth

$\frac{1}{8}$ teaspoon ground black pepper

  1 small bulb fennel (about $\frac{1}{2}$ pound), trimmed and sliced (about 2 cups)

  1 medium onion, chopped (about $\frac{1}{2}$ cup)

  2 cloves garlic, minced

  1 package (10 ounces) frozen leaf spinach

  1 can (14$\frac{1}{2}$ ounces) diced tomatoes

  1 can (15 ounces) white kidney (cannellini) beans, undrained

PLACE broth, black pepper, fennel, onion and garlic in 5$\frac{1}{2}$- to 6-quart slow cooker.

COVER and cook on LOW 6 to 7 hours.

ADD spinach, tomatoes and beans. Turn heat to HIGH. Cover and cook 1 hour.

Serves 6.

Hearty Pork Stew

Prep Time: 25 minutes
Cook Time: 7 to 8 hours

2 pounds sweet potatoes, peeled and cut into 2-inch pieces
    (about 2 cups)

2 pounds boneless pork shoulder roast, cut into 1-inch pieces

1 can (14½ ounces) Campbell's® Chicken Gravy

1 teaspoon dried thyme leaves, crushed

½ teaspoon crushed red pepper

1 can (15 ounces) black-eyed peas, rinsed and drained

PLACE potatoes in 4- to 6-quart slow cooker. Top with pork.

MIX gravy, thyme, red pepper and peas. Pour over pork and potatoes.

COVER and cook on LOW 7 to 8 hours* or until pork is fork-tender.

Serves 8.

Or on HIGH 4 to 5 hours

TIP:
Freeze leftovers of this hearty stew as individual portions. Just reheat in a
microwave for fast weeknight dinners!

Slow Cooker Beef & Mushroom Stew

Prep Time: 20 minutes
Cook Time: 10 to 12 hours

1½ pounds boneless beef bottom round **or** chuck roast, cut into 1-inch pieces

Ground black pepper

¼ cup all-purpose flour

2 tablespoons vegetable oil

1 can (10½ ounces) Campbell's® Condensed French Onion Soup

1 cup Burgundy **or** other dry red wine

2 cloves garlic, minced

1 teaspoon dried Italian seasoning, crushed

3 cups mushrooms, cut in half (about 10 ounces)

3 medium carrots (about ½ pound), cut into 2-inch pieces

1 cup frozen small whole white onions

¼ cup water

SPRINKLE beef with black pepper and coat with **2 tablespoons** flour. Heat oil in large skillet over medium-high heat. Add beef and cook until browned, stirring often.

MIX beef, soup, wine, garlic, Italian seasoning, garlic, mushrooms, carrots and onions in 3½-quart slow cooker.

COVER and cook on LOW 10 to 12 hours* or until beef is fork-tender.

MIX remaining flour and water. Stir flour mixture into cooker. Turn heat to HIGH. Cover and cook 15 minutes or until slightly thickened.

Serves 6.

*Or on HIGH for 4 to 5 hours

Hearty Mixed Bean Stew with Sausage

Prep Time: 15 minutes
Cook Time: 8 to 9 hours

¾ pound sweet Italian pork sausage, casing removed

10 cups Swanson® Chicken **or** Natural Goodness™ Chicken Broth

¼ teaspoon ground black pepper

2 medium carrots, chopped (about ⅔ cup)

1 stalk celery, chopped (about ½ cup)

4 ounces dried pinto beans (about ¾ cup)

4 ounces dried navy beans (about ¾ cup)

4 ounces dried kidney beans (about ¾ cup)

6 sun-dried tomatoes in oil, drained and thinly sliced (about ¼ cup)

Grated Parmesan cheese

COOK sausage in medium skillet over medium-high heat until sausage is browned, stirring to separate meat. Place in 5- to 5½-quart slow cooker.

ADD broth, black pepper, carrots, celery and pinto, navy and kidney beans.

COVER and cook on LOW 7 to 8 hours*.

STIR in tomatoes. Cover and cook 1 hour or until beans are tender. Serve with cheese.

Serves 8.

*Or on HIGH 4 to 4 1/2 hours

Chipotle Chili

Prep Time: 15 minutes
Cook Time: 8 to 9 hours

1 jar (16 ounces) Pace® Chipotle Chunky Salsa

1 cup water

2 tablespoons chili powder

1 large onion, chopped (about 1 cup)

2 pounds beef for stew, cut into ½-inch pieces

1 can (about 19 ounces) red kidney beans, drained

Shredded Cheddar cheese (optional)

Sour cream (optional)

MIX salsa, water, chili powder, onion, beef and beans in 3½-quart slow cooker.

COVER and cook on LOW 8 to 9 hours* or until beef is fork-tender. Serve with cheese and sour cream, if desired.

Serves 8.

*Or on HIGH 4 to 5 hours

TIP:
Serve with savory corn muffins made from your favorite corn muffin mix and Swanson® Broth. Follow package directions, substituting an equal amount of broth for the milk.

Hearty Beef Stew

Prep Time: 20 minutes
Cook Time: 10 to 12 hours

1½   pounds beef for stew, cut into 1-inch pieces

    Ground black pepper

¼   cup all-purpose flour

1   tablespoon vegetable oil

2½   cups cubed potatoes

4   medium carrots, sliced (about 2 cups)

2   medium onions, cut into wedges

4   cloves garlic, minced

3   cups Swanson® Beef **or** Lower Sodium Beef Broth

1   tablespoon Worcestershire sauce

1   teaspoon dried thyme leaves, crushed

1   bay leaf

¼   cup water

1   cup frozen peas

SPRINKLE beef with black pepper and coat with **2 tablespoons** flour. Heat oil in large skillet over medium-high heat. Add beef and cook until browned, stirring often.

PLACE potatoes, carrots, onions and garlic in 3½-quart slow cooker. Top with beef. Add broth, Worcestershire, thyme and bay leaf.

COVER and cook on LOW 10 to 12 hours* or until beef is fork-tender. Remove bay leaf.

MIX remaining flour and water. Add flour mixture and peas to cooker. Turn heat to HIGH. Cover and cook 15 minutes or until slightly thickened.

Serves 6.

*Or cook on HIGH 5 to 6 hours

Greek-Style Beef Stew

Prep Time: 10 minutes
Cook Time: 8 to 10 hours

2- to 2½-pound boneless beef bottom round **or** chuck pot roast, cut into 1-inch pieces

1 bag (16 ounces) frozen small white onions (about 4 cups)

1 bag (16 ounces) fresh **or** frozen whole baby carrots (about 2½ cups)

2 tablespoons all-purpose flour

1 can (14 ounces) Swanson® Beef **or** Lower Sodium Beef Broth (1¾ cups)

1 can (5.5 ounces) V8® Vegetable Juice

1 tablespoon packed brown sugar

Bouquet Garni

Hot buttered noodles

PLACE beef, onions and carrots to 3½- to 6-quart slow cooker. Sprinkle with flour and toss to coat.

MIX broth, vegetable juice and brown sugar. Pour over beef and vegetables. Submerge *Bouquet Garni* into broth mixture.

COVER and cook on LOW 8 to 10 hours* or until beef is fork-tender. Remove Bouquet Garni. Serve over noodles.

Serves 6.

Or on HIGH 4 to 5 hours

Bouquet Garni: Lay a **4-inch square of cheesecloth** flat on counter. Place **½ teaspoon** whole cloves, **1** cinnamon stick and **1** bay leaf in center of cloth. Bring corners of cheesecloth together into a bundle and tie with kitchen string.

Not Your Gramma's Kugel
Recipe on page 52

Heritage Recipes

Slow cooking is the perfect method for preparing many of the traditional, home-style dishes we all grew up with. What makes it so ideal? Sheer ease and convenience. Today's slow cookers skip the lengthy stovetop simmering, laborious stirring, and constant attention required in the past. Yet they faithfully reproduce the same wonderful results: fork-tender meats and poultry, succulent vegetables, and concentrated sauces brimming with flavor.

Slow cookers also do an excellent job of recreating scrumptious desserts like gramma used to make—from dense bread pudding to moist spice cake. So celebrate our food heritage with these familiar recipes and discover just how easy it is to make tasty classics the slow cooker way.

Herbed Turkey Breast

Prep Time: 10 minutes
Cook Time: 8 to 9 hours
Stand Time: 10 minutes

1 can (10¾ ounces) Campbell's® Condensed Cream of Mushroom **or** 98% Fat Free Cream of Mushroom Soup

½ cup water

4½- to 5-pound turkey breast

1 teaspoon poultry seasoning

1 tablespoon chopped fresh parsley

Hot mashed potatoes

MIX soup and water in 3½- to 6-quart slow cooker. Rinse turkey with cold water and pat dry. Rub turkey with poultry seasoning and place in cooker. Sprinkle with parsley.

COVER and cook on LOW 8 to 9 hours*. Insert meat thermometer into thickest part of meat, without touching bone, to check for doneness. Cook until thermometer reads 170°F. Let stand 10 minutes before slicing. Serve with mashed potatoes.

Serves 8.

*Or on HIGH 4 to 5 hours

TIP:
If using a frozen turkey breast, thaw before cooking.

Apricot-Glazed Pork Roast

Prep Time: 5 minutes
Cook Time: 8 to 9 hours

1 can (10½ ounces) Campbell's® Condensed Chicken Broth

1 jar (18 ounces) apricot preserves

2 tablespoons Dijon-style mustard

1 large onion, chopped (about 1 cup)

   3½- to 4-pound boneless pork loin

MIX broth, preserves, mustard and onion in 3½-quart slow cooker. Cut pork to fit. Add to cooker.

COVER and cook on LOW 8 to 9 hours* or until pork is no longer pink.

Serves 8.

*Or on HIGH 4 to 5 hours

For thicker sauce, mix **2 tablespoons** cornstarch and **2 tablespoons** water until smooth. Remove pork from cooker. Stir cornstarch mixture into cooker. Turn heat to HIGH. Cover and cook 10 minutes or until mixture boils and thickens.

TIP:
Use some of the glaze from the roast for a delicious mashed potato topping.

Chocolate Almond Bread
Pudding with Dried Cherries

Prep Time: 10 minutes
Cook Time: 2½ to 3 hours

Vegetable cooking spray

10 slices Pepperidge Farm® White Sandwich Bread, cut into cubes (about 5 cups)

½ cup dried cherries, chopped

½ cup semi-sweet chocolate pieces

1¾ cups milk

½ cup sugar

⅓ cup unsweetened baking cocoa

½ teaspoon almond **or** vanilla extract

4 eggs, beaten

Sweetened whipped cream (optional)

Toasted almonds (optional)

SPRAY inside of 4½- to 5-quart slow cooker with cooking spray.

PLACE bread cubes in slow cooker. Sprinkle with cherries and chocolate.

MIX milk, sugar, cocoa, vanilla and eggs. Pour over bread mixture. Stir and push bread cubes into milk mixture to coat.

COVER and cook on LOW 2½ to 3 hours or until set. Serve warm with whipped cream and almonds, if desired.

Serves 6.

Raisin Cinnamon Bread Pudding

Prep Time: 10 minutes
Cook Time: 2½ to 3 hours

Vegetable cooking spray

10 slices Pepperidge Farm® Raisin Cinnamon Swirl Bread, cut into cubes (about 5 cups)

1 can (14 ounces) sweetened condensed milk

1 cup water

1 teaspoon vanilla extract

4 eggs, beaten

Ice cream (optional)

SPRAY inside of 4½ - to 5-quart slow cooker with cooking spray.

PLACE bread cubes in slow cooker.

MIX milk, water, vanilla and eggs. Pour over bread. Stir and push bread cubes into milk mixture to coat.

COVER and cook on LOW 2½ to 3 hours or until set. Serve warm with ice cream, if desired.

Serves 6.

TIP:
Even when it's too hot to bake, you can surprise your family with fresh, homemade desserts made in the slow cooker.

Brown Sugar Spice Cake

Prep Time: 10 minutes
Cook Time: 2½ to 3 hours

    Vegetable cooking spray

1 can (10¾ ounces) Campbell's® Condensed Tomato Soup

½ cup water

2 eggs

1 box (about 18 ounces) spice cake mix

1¼ cups hot water

¾ cup packed brown sugar

1 teaspoon ground cinnamon

    Vanilla ice cream

SPRAY inside of 3½- to 4-quart slow cooker with cooking spray.

MIX soup, water, eggs and cake mix according to package directions. Pour batter into slow cooker.

MIX water, brown sugar and cinnamon. Pour over batter.

COVER and cook on HIGH 2 to 2½ hours or until toothpick inserted in center comes out clean.

SPOON warm cake into bowls, scooping sauce from bottom of cooker. Serve warm with ice cream.

Serves 8.

TIP:
This is a great dessert to make when you're entertaining and the oven is occupied with another dish.

Slow-Cooked Autumn Brisket

Prep Time: 20 minutes
Cook Time: 8 to 9 hours

   3-pound boneless beef brisket

1 small head cabbage (about 1 pound), cut into 8 wedges

1 large sweet potato (about ¾ pound), peeled and cut into 1-inch pieces

1 large onion, cut into 8 wedges

1 medium Granny Smith apple, cored and cut into 8 wedges

2 cans (10¾ ounces **each**) Campbell's® Condensed Cream of Celery **or** 98% Fat Free Cream of Celery Soup

1 cup water

2 teaspoons caraway seed (optional)

SPRINKLE brisket with seasonings, as desired. Place brisket in 6-quart slow cooker. Top with cabbage, sweet potato, onion and apple. Mix soup, water and caraway, if desired. Pour over brisket and vegetable mixture.

COVER and cook on LOW 8 to 9 hours* or until brisket is fork-tender.

Serves 8.

*Or on HIGH 4 to 5 hours

TIP:
Try to buy roasts and other large cuts of meat that fit into your slow cooker, or plan on trimming them to fit.

Slow Cooker Chicken & Dumplings

Prep Time: 20 minutes
Cook Time: 7 to 8 hours 30 minutes

2 medium Yukon Gold potatoes, cut into 1-inch pieces (about 2 cups)

2 cups fresh **or** frozen whole baby carrots

2 stalks celery, sliced (about 1 cup)

1½ pounds skinless, boneless chicken breasts, cut into 1-inch pieces

2 cans (10¾ ounces **each**) Campbell's® Condensed Cream of Chicken **or** 98% Fat Free Cream of Chicken Soup

1 cup water

1 teaspoon dried thyme leaves, crushed

¼ teaspoon ground black pepper

2 cups all-purpose baking mix

⅔ cup milk

PLACE potatoes, carrots, celery and chicken in 6-quart slow cooker.

MIX soup, water, thyme and black pepper. Pour over chicken and vegetables.

COVER and cook on LOW 7 to 8 hours* or until chicken is no longer pink.

MIX baking mix and milk. Spoon batter over chicken mixture. Turn heat to HIGH. Tilt lid to vent and cook 30 minutes or until dumplings are cooked in center.

Serves 8.

*Or on HIGH 4 to 5 hours

TIP:
Leaving the lid slightly ajar while cooking the dumplings prevents condensation from dripping onto the food.

Ham & Scalloped Potato Casserole

Prep Time: 25 minutes
Cook Time: 7 to 8 hours

Vegetable cooking spray

4 pounds potatoes, peeled and thinly sliced (about 8 cups)

1 pound diced cooked ham (2 cups)

1 large onion, sliced (about 1 cup)

2 cans (10¾ ounces **each**) Campbell's® Condensed Cheddar Cheese Soup

1 cup milk

1 teaspoon paprika

SPRAY inside of 5- to 6-quart slow cooker with cooking spray.

LAYER potatoes, ham and onions in cooker.

MIX soup and milk and pour over vegetable mixture. Sprinkle with paprika.

COVER and cook on LOW 7 to 8 hours*.

Serves 8.

*Or on HIGH 4 to 5 hours

TIP:
Serve this classic country casserole with applesauce and a tossed salad.

Country-Style Ribs

Prep Time: 25 minutes
Cook Time: 7 to 8 hours

4 pounds pork country-style ribs, cut into serving pieces

Ground black pepper

3 cloves garlic, minced

1 can (10¾ ounces) Campbell's® Condensed Tomato Soup

2 tablespoons packed brown sugar

2 tablespoons cider vinegar

1 tablespoon Worcestershire sauce

2 teaspoons dry mustard

SPRINKLE ribs with black pepper.

BROWN ribs in 2 batches in large nonstick skillet over medium-high heat. Place ribs in 5- to 6-quart slow cooker and sprinkle with garlic.

MIX soup, brown sugar, vinegar, Worcestershire and mustard. Pour over ribs and toss to coat.

COVER and cook on LOW 7 to 8 hours*.

Serves 8.

*Or on HIGH 4 to 5 hours

TIP:
Ribs also can be cooked without the browning step. Use a spoon to remove fat from sauce before serving.

Beef Bourguignonne
Recipe on page 72

A World of Flavors

Slow cooking is more than just a convenient way to prepare familiar comfort foods and family favorites. If you enjoy trying foods from other countries or experimenting with regional flavors, the slow cooker is a perfect travel partner!

Whether you have a yen for Asian or crave some Cajun spice, your slow cooker can prepare just about any type of meal you can imagine and deliver authentic-tasting results. This collection of international recipes features the predominant flavors of several of today's most popular ethnic and regional cuisines. By preparing these dishes in your slow cooker, you'll make it easy as well as fun for your family to get adventurous.

Beef Bourguignonne

(pictured on page 70)

Prep Time: 10 minutes
Cook Time: 8 to 9 hours

1 can (10¾ ounces) Campbell's® Condensed Golden Mushroom Soup

1 cup Burgundy **or** other dry red wine

2 cloves garlic, minced

1 teaspoon dried thyme leaves, crushed

2 cups small button mushrooms (about 6 ounces)

2 cups fresh **or** frozen whole baby carrots

1 cup frozen small whole onions

1½ pounds beef top round steak, 1½-inches thick, cut into 1-inch pieces

MIX soup, wine, garlic, thyme, mushrooms, carrots, onions and beef in 3½-quart slow cooker.

COVER and cook on LOW 8 to 9 hours* or until beef is fork-tender.

Serves 6.

*Or on HIGH for 4 to 5 hours

TIP:
Slow cookers work best half full to three-quarters full, so go ahead and fill it up. Freeze the leftovers for another meal.

Slow Cooker Swiss Steak

Prep Time: 15 minutes
Cook Time: 8 to 10 hours

1½ pounds boneless beef round steak, cut into 6 pieces

6 to 8 new potatoes (about ½ pound), cut into quarters

1½ cups fresh **or** frozen whole baby carrots

1 medium onion, sliced (about ½ cup)

1 can (14½ ounces) diced tomatoes with basil, garlic and oregano

1 can (10¼ ounces) Campbell's® Beef Gravy

COOK beef in 2 batches in large nonstick skillet over medium-high heat until browned.

PLACE beef, potatoes, carrots and onion in 3½-quart slow cooker. Mix tomatoes and gravy. Pour over beef and vegetables.

COVER and cook on LOW 8 to 10 hours* or until beef is fork-tender.

Serves 6.

*Or on HIGH 4 to 5 hours

TIP:
Slow cooking actually tenderizes less-expensive cuts of meat like round steak, so you save time, effort, and money.

Creamy Blush Sauce with Turkey and Penne

Prep Time: 10 minutes
Cook Time: 7 to 8 hours

4 turkey thighs, skin removed (about 3 pounds)

1 jar (1 pound 9.75 ounces) Prego® Mushroom & Green Pepper Pasta Sauce

½ teaspoon crushed red pepper

½ cup half-and-half

Hot cooked penne pasta

Grated Parmesan cheese

PLACE turkey in 3½- to 5-quart slow cooker. Pour pasta sauce over turkey and sprinkle with pepper.

COVER and cook on LOW 7 to 8 hours*. Remove turkey and keep warm.

ADD half-and-half to cooker. Spoon sauce over turkey and pasta. Sprinkle with cheese.

Serves 8.

*Or on HIGH 4 to 5 hours

TIP:
Substitute 8 chicken thighs (about 2 pounds) for the turkey thighs. Serves 6.

Coq Au Vin

Prep Time: 10 minutes
Cook Time: 8 to 10 hours

1 package (10 ounces) sliced mushrooms (about 4 cups)

1 bag (16 ounces) frozen small white onions (about 4 cups)

2- to 2½-pounds skinless, boneless chicken (combination of thighs and breasts), cut into 1-inch strips

¼ cup cornstarch

1 can (10¾ ounces) Campbell's® Condensed Golden Mushroom Soup

1 cup Burgundy **or** other dry red wine

1 sprig fresh rosemary

Hot mashed **or** oven-roasted potatoes

PLACE mushrooms, onions, rosemary and chicken in 3½-quart slow cooker.

MIX cornstarch, soup and wine until smooth. Pour over chicken and vegetables.

COVER and cook on LOW for 8 to 10 hours*. Remove rosemary sprig. Serve with potatoes.

Serves 6.

*Or on HIGH 4 to 5 hours

Jambalaya

Prep Time: 15 minutes
Cook Time: 7 to 8 hours 40 minutes

2 cups Swanson® Chicken **or** Natural Goodness™ Chicken Broth

1 tablespoon Creole seasoning

1 large green pepper, diced (about 1⅓ cups)

1 large onion, diced (about 1 cup)

2 large celery stalks, diced (about 1 cup)

1 can (about 14½ ounces) diced tomatoes

1 pound kielbasa, diced

¾ pound skinless, boneless chicken thighs, cut into cubes

1 cup **uncooked** regular long-grain white rice

½ pound fresh medium shrimp, shelled and deveined

MIX broth, Creole seasoning, pepper, onion, celery, tomatoes, kielbasa, chicken and rice in 3½- to 6-quart slow cooker.

COVER and cook on LOW 7 to 8 hours*.

ADD shrimp. Cover and cook for 40 minutes or until done.

Serves 6.

*Or on HIGH 4 to 5 hours

Beef Taco Casserole

Prep Time: 10 minutes
Cook Time: 7 to 8 hours

2 pounds ground beef

1 can (10¾ ounces) Campbell's® Condensed Creamy Tomato Ranchero Soup

½ cup water

1 can (14½ ounces) diced tomatoes with green chilies

8 corn tortillas (6-inch), cut into ½-inch strips

1 cup shredded Cheddar cheese (4 ounces)

3 green onions, chopped (about ⅓ cup)

Sour cream

COOK beef in 2 batches in large skillet over medium-high heat, stirring to separate meat. Pour off fat.

MIX beef, soup, water, tomatoes and tortillas in 3½- to 5-quart slow cooker.

COVER and cook on LOW 7 to 8 hours*. Stir in cheese. Cover and cook 5 minutes. Sprinkle with green onions and serve with sour cream.

Serves 8.

*Or on HIGH 4 to 5 hours

Ratatouille with Penne

Prep Time: 15 minutes
Cook Time: 5½ to 6 hours

1 can (10¾ ounces) Campbell's® Condensed Tomato Soup

1 tablespoon olive oil

⅛ teaspoon ground black pepper

1 small eggplant, peeled and cut into ½-inch cubes (about 5 cups)

1 medium zucchini, thinly sliced (about 1½ cups)

1 medium red pepper, diced (about 1 cup)

1 large onion, sliced (about 1 cup)

1 clove garlic, minced

Hot cooked penne pasta

Grated Parmesan cheese (optional)

MIX soup, olive oil, black pepper, eggplant, zucchini, red pepper, onion and garlic in 4- to 5½-quart slow cooker.

COVER and cook on LOW 5½ to 6 hours* or until vegetables are tender.

SERVE over pasta. Serve with cheese, if desired.

Serves 4.

*Or on HIGH 2½ to 3 hours

TIP:
Serve with Pepperidge Farm® Hot & Crusty Italian Bread.

Mexican Black Bean and Beef Soup

Prep Time: 10 minutes
Cook Time: 8 to 9 hours

2 cups water

1 jar (16 ounces) Pace® Chunky Salsa, any variety

1 tablespoon chopped fresh cilantro leaves

1 teaspoon ground cumin

1 large onion, chopped (about 1 cup)

1 cup frozen whole kernel corn

1 can (about 15 ounces) black beans, drained

1 pound beef for stew, cut into ½-inch pieces

MIX water, salsa, cilantro, cumin, onion, corn, beans and beef in 3½- to 6-quart slow cooker.

COVER and cook on LOW 8 to 9 hours* or until beef is fork-tender.

Serves 8.

Or on HIGH 4 to 5 hours

TIP:
Serve with a mixed green salad and warm flour or corn tortillas.

Chicken Cacciatore

Prep Time: 10 minutes
Cook Time: 7 to 8 hours 10 minutes

1 can (14 ounces) Swanson® Chicken **or** Natural Goodness™ Chicken Broth (1¾ cups)

1 teaspoon garlic powder

2 cans (14½ ounces **each**) diced Italian-style tomatoes

4 cups mushrooms, cut in half (about 12 ounces)

2 large onions, chopped (about 2 cups)

3 pounds chicken parts, skin removed

Hot cooked spaghetti

MIX broth, garlic powder, tomatoes, mushrooms, onions in 3½-quart slow cooker. Add chicken and turn to coat.

COVER and cook on LOW 7 to 8 hours* or until chicken is no longer pink. Serve over spaghetti.

Serves 6.

*Or on HIGH 4 to 5 hours

For thicker sauce, mix **2 tablespoons** cornstarch and **2 tablespoons** water until smooth. Remove chicken from cooker. Stir cornstarch mixture into cooker. Turn heat to HIGH. Cover and cook 10 minutes or until mixture boils and thickens.

TIP:
Make Simple Seasoned Pasta instead of spaghetti. Bring 2 cans of Swanson® Chicken Broth with Italian Herbs to a boil. Stir in 3 cups uncooked corkscrew pasta. Simmer gently over medium heat 10 minutes or until pasta is done and mixture is saucy.

Chicken and Rice Pacifica

Prep Time: 20 minutes
Cook Time: 7 to 8 hours

2 cans (10½ ounces **each**) Campbell's® Condensed Chicken Broth

1 cup water

¼ cup soy sauce

2 cloves garlic, minced

1 medium green **or** red pepper, cut into 1½-inch pieces (about 1 cup)

4 green onions, cut into 2-inch pieces (about 1 cup)

1 can (20 ounces) pineapple chunks in juice

1 cup **uncooked** regular long-grain white rice

8 skinless, boneless chicken thighs (about 2 pounds), cut into 1½-inch pieces

Toasted sliced almonds

MIX broth, water, soy, garlic, chicken, pepper, green onions, pineapple with juice, rice and chicken in 6-quart slow cooker.

COVER and cook on LOW 7 to 8 hours* or until chicken is no longer pink. Sprinkle with almonds before serving.

Serves 8.

*Or on HIGH 4 to 5 hours

TIP:
To toast almonds, arrange almonds in single layer in a shallow baking pan. Bake at 350°F. for 10 minutes or until lightly browned.

Asian Tomato Beef

Prep Time: 10 minutes
Cook Time: 7 to 8 hours 15 minutes

2 cans (10¾ ounces **each**) Campbell's® Condensed Tomato Soup

⅓ cup soy sauce

⅓ cup vinegar

1½ teaspoons garlic powder

¼ teaspoon ground black pepper

3- to 3½-pound boneless beef round steak, cut into strips

6 cups broccoli flowerets

Hot cooked rice

MIX soup, soy, vinegar, garlic powder, black pepper and beef in 3½-quart slow cooker.

COVER and cook on LOW 7 to 8 hours* or until beef is fork-tender.

STIR mixture. Add broccoli. Turn heat to HIGH. Cover and cook 15 minutes or until broccoli is tender-crisp. Serve over rice.

Serves 8.

*Or on HIGH 4 to 5 hours

TIP:
Continue the Asian theme right through dessert. Slice and lightly toast pound cake. Top with canned mandarin oranges in syrup and slivered almonds.

Zesty Slow Cooker Italian Pot Roast

Prep Time: 45 minutes
Cook Time: 10 to 12 hours

4 medium potatoes (about 1 pound), cut into quarters

2 cups fresh **or** frozen whole baby carrots

1 stalk celery, cut into 1-inch pieces

1 medium Italian plum tomato, diced

2½-pound boneless beef bottom round **or** chuck pot roast

½ teaspoon ground black pepper

1 can (10¾ ounces) Campbell's® Condensed Tomato Soup

½ cup water

1 tablespoon chopped roasted garlic* **or** fresh garlic

1 teaspoon **each** dried basil leaves, dried oregano leaves **and** dried parsley flakes, crushed

1 teaspoon vinegar

PLACE potatoes, carrots, celery and tomato in 3½-quart slow cooker. Sprinkle roast with black pepper and place on top.

MIX soup, water, garlic, basil, oregano, parsley flakes and vinegar. Pour over roast and vegetables.

COVER and cook on LOW 10 to 12 hours** or until roast is fork-tender.

Serves 4 to 6.

For thicker gravy, mix **¼ cup** all-purpose flour and **½ cup** water. Remove roast from cooker. Stir flour mixture into cooker. Turn heat to HIGH. Cover and cook 10 minutes or until mixture boils and thickens.

*To roast garlic, place whole garlic bulb on piece of aluminum foil. Drizzle with vegetable oil and wrap. Roast at 350°F. for 45 minutes or until soft. Peel and chop garlic.

**Or on HIGH 5 to 6 hours

Slow Cooker Tuscan Beef Stew

Prep Time: 5 minutes
Cook Time: 8 to 9 hours

1 can (10¾ ounces) Campbell's® Condensed Tomato Soup

1 can (10½ ounces) Campbell's® Condensed Beef Broth

½ cup Burgundy or other dry red wine **or** water

1 teaspoon dried Italian seasoning, crushed

½ teaspoon garlic powder

1 can (14½ ounces) diced Italian-style tomatoes

3 large carrots (about ¾ pound), cut into 1-inch pieces

2 pounds beef for stew, cut into 1-inch pieces

2 cans (about 16 ounces **each**) white kidney (cannellini) beans, drained

MIX soup, broth, wine, Italian seasoning, garlic powder, tomatoes, carrots and beef in 3½-quart slow cooker.

COVER and cook on LOW 8 to 9 hours* or until beef is fork-tender.

STIR in beans. Turn heat to HIGH. Cook 10 minutes.

Serves 8.

*Or on HIGH 4 to 5 hours

TIP:
Egg noodles are a lovely complement to this stew.

Index

Apricot-Glazed Pork Roast 56

Asian Tomato Beef 88

Barley and Lentil Soup 30

Beef

Asian Tomato Beef 88

Beef Bourguignonne 72

Beef Taco Casserole.....................80

Beef & Vegetable Soup 29

Chipotle Chili 46

Greek-Style Beef Stew 48

Hearty Beef Stew 47

Melt-in-Your-Mouth Short
Ribs 22

Mexican Black Bean and Beef
Soup 84

Slow-Cooked Autumn
Brisket 64

Slow Cooker Beef
& Mushroom Stew 42

Slow Cooker Swiss Steak 73

Slow Cooker Tuscan Beef
Stew...................................90

Spiced Pot Roast 53

Weekday Pot Roast &
Vegetables 11

Zesty Slow Cooker Italian
Pot Roast 89

Beef Bourguignonne 72

Beef Taco Casserole 80

Beef & Vegetable Soup 29

Brown Sugar Spice Cake 62

Chicken

Chicken and Rice Pacifica 86

Chicken Cacciatore 85

Chicken in Creamy Sun-Dried-
Tomato Sauce...........................10

Coq Au Vin 76

Creamy Chicken & Wild Rice 20

Creamy Chicken Tortilla Soup 28

Golden Chicken with Noodles 16

Jambalaya 78

Nacho Chicken & Rice Wraps........21

Orange Chicken with Green
Onions and Walnuts 14

Slow Cooker Chicken
& Dumplings 66

Slow-Simmered Chicken Rice
Soup 36

Southwestern Chicken & White
Bean Soup..............................32

Chicken and Rice Pacifica...................86

Chicken Cacciatore 85

Chicken in Creamy Sun-Dried-
Tomato Sauce...........................10

Chipotle Chili.................................46

Chocolate Almond Bread Pudding
with Dried Cherries 58

Coq Au Vin 76

Country-Style Ribs 69

Creamy Blush Sauce with Turkey
and Penne 74

Creamy Chicken Tortilla Soup.............28

Creamy Chicken & Wild Rice.............20

Desserts

Brown Sugar Spice Cake.................62

Chocolate Almond Bread
Pudding with Dried Cherries 58

Raisin Cinnamon Bread
Pudding.................................60

Golden Chicken with Noodles............16

Golden Mushroom Pork
& Apples..............................18

Greek-Style Beef Stew........................48

Ham & Scalloped Potato
Casserole..68

Hearty Beef Stew 47

Hearty Mixed Bean Stew with
Sausage 44

Hearty Pork Stew 40

Herbed Turkey Breast........................54

Jambalaya 78

Melt-in-Your-Mouth Short
Ribs 22

Mexican Black Bean and Beef
Soup 84

Nacho Chicken & Rice Wraps 21

Not Your Gramma's Kugel 52

Orange Chicken with Green
Onions and Walnuts 14

Index

Pork

Apricot-Glazed Pork Roast 56

Country-Style Ribs.........................69

Golden Mushroom Pork
   & Apples.....................................18

Ham & Scalloped Potato
   Casserole.....................................68

Hearty Mixed Bean Stew with
   Sausage 44

Hearty Pork Stew..........................40

Jambalaya 78

Slow-Cooked Pulled Pork
   Sandwiches.................................12

Raisin Cinnamon Bread
   Pudding..60

Ratatouille with Penne 82

Slow-Cooked Autumn Brisket 64

Slow-Cooked Pulled Pork
   Sandwiches......................................12

Slow Cooker Beef &
   Mushroom Stew 42

Slow Cooker Chicken
   & Dumplings 66

Slow Cooker Swiss Steak 73

Slow Cooker Tuscan Beef
   Stew...90

Slow-Simmered Chicken Rice
   Soup 36

Southwestern Bean Medley 24

Southwestern Chicken & White
   Bean Soup.......................................32

Spiced Pot Roast...............................53

Turkey

Creamy Blush Sauce with Turkey
   and Penne 74

Herbed Turkey Breast 54

Veal Stew with Garden Vegetables 34

Vegetarian

Ratatouille with Penne 82

Southwestern Bean Medley.............24

White Bean with Fennel Soup.........38

Weekday Pot Roast & Vegetables........11

White Bean with Fennel Soup 38

Zesty Slow Cooker Italian Pot
   Roast 89